The Big Guy Upstairs by Mary Vine
Illustrated by Brenna Tedesco
Melland Publishing

THE BIG GUY UPSTAIRS by Mary Vine

ILLUSTRATED by Brenna Tedesco

COPYRIGHT © 2015 by Mary Vine

Contact Information: authormaryvine@gmail.com

Melland Publishing
2015
Calawell, ID 83607

ISBN-13: 978-0-9966876-0-7 (Paperback)
Library of Congress Control Number: 2015913319

First Paperback Edition: 2015

Published in the United States of America
Melland Publishing

"Mrs. Wilson is sick? Well, I will say a prayer to the Big Guy Upstairs for her. Take care."

Johnny looked up from his coloring book as Grandma set down her phone. "Grandma, who is the Big Guy Upstairs?" he asked.

3

"Oh, that's just what people say sometimes. It means God."

"The Big Guy Upstairs is God?"

"Yes," she said, taking vegetables out of the refrigerator. "I think I will make some soup."

5

Johnny nodded and then closed the coloring book. "I'm going to get my spy magnifying glass."

"You have a mystery to solve, huh? That sounds like a fine start to the day. I saw it next to the toy box," said Grandma with a smile.

"1, 2, 3, 4, 5, 6, 7, 8, 9, 10, 11, 13, 15, 20," counted Johnny as he climbed the stairs. Finally, he made it to the attic door at the top of the steps. He'd never been in Grandma's attic, so that was probably why he hadn't seen God yet.

Johnny turned the knob and opened the door, and stood on his tip toes to flip up the light switch.

"God, are you in here?" he asked, with the spy glass to his eye.

Johnny looked around. "There's lots of boxes and stuff all over. How can I find you? Oh boy, is that a pirate's trunk over there? Maybe with some treasure in it?"

He could barely hear Grandma calling him.
"Johnny, what are you doing?"

"I'm coming!" Down the stairs he went,
saying, "1, 2, 3, 4, 5, 6, 7, 8, 9, 10, 11, 16, 23,
um... I don't remember what's next."

Grandma held a mixing bowl and a wooden
spoon. "Johnny, I need you to mix the
brownies."

"I know you make good brownies. Now, just set your spy glass down, and when you're done you can go back to being a detective."

Grandma put the bowl on the table and Johnny sat on his knees in the chair so he could reach the bowl and stir the brownies. She went back to stirring a pot at the stove.

"I mixed the batter 123 times," he said, and tried to sneak away real fast so Grand-ma wouldn't clean his face.

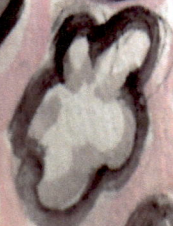

13

"Okay, step number 1, 2, 3, 4, 5, 6, 7, 8, 9, 10, 11, 16, 20, 22."

"God, are you in there?" asked Johnny. "Can you come out? Grandma needs to talk to you about Mrs. Wilson. She's sick or something."

Johnny wondered if there could be any toys up here. He forgets where he puts his toys sometimes, so maybe Grandma forgot some, too. Maybe that was what God was doing in the attic. He probably liked super heroes, too, and they could play together.

15

"We can play. I'll open the chest and we can look for the treasure."

But, there wasn't any treasure inside, or toys, only some of Grandma's dresses.

"Johnny! Oh, there you are. What did you find with your spy magnifying glass?"

"I'm looking for super hero toys."

Grandma tapped her chin with a finger. "I didn't pack any toys away up here."

"Oh," said Johnny, looking rather disappointed, then he smiled as if remembering something important. "I'm upstairs looking for God. For the Big Guy Upstairs."

19

"God doesn't live in the attic. He is like a super hero that you can't see with your eyes," said Grandma with a chuckle and led Johnny to the window where they looked down at the countryside.

"Wow."

"See the mountain, hills, and animals below? God made everything you see out this window, so He has more power than any super hero. He loves and cheers for us, and knows all of our names, even yours, Johnny. He wants us to love and believe in Him, and love and help other people when they need it."

"Where does He live, then?"

"In our hearts," answered Grandma.

"In our hearts?" asked Johnny patting his chest. "I think I feel it, because I feel happy inside my heart."

"I think you are right."

"Can we help Mrs. Wilson?" he asked.

"That's just what I was thinking. Let's take her some soup and brownies. She is too sick to cook, and we have plenty to share."

"She'll like my brownies," said Johnny.

"I know she will."

THE END

## ABOUT THE AUTHOR

Author Mary Vine is a multi-published fiction author currently writing a mix of romance with a bit of suspense-and a bit of inspiration. Besides writing, Mary works as a licensed speech language pathology assistant, teaching individual and small groups of children, ages kindergarten through twelfth grades. THE BIG GUY UPSTAIRS is Mary's debut children's book. Readers can learn more about her work at www.maryvine.com.

## ABOUT THE ILLUSTRATOR

Brenna Tedesco is a freelance illustrator from the Boston area. This fall, Miss Tedesco will begin her freshman year at Massachusetts College of Art and Design majoring in illustration. In addition to freelance work, Brenna runs an Instagram account entitled art_forever219 and a Redbubble shop under Ethereal Daydreams. Looking to the future, Brenna hopes to illustrate many more books and foster a love of reading in children across the globe.

www.ingramcontent.com/pod-product-compliance
Lightning Source LLC
Chambersburg PA
CBHW042058040426
42447CB00003B/268